ISLAM, TERRORISM AND THE MIDDLE EAST

By

John J. Davis, Th.D., D.D.

PO Box 557 • Winona Lake, IN 46590

The chapters of this book originally appeared as series of feature articles in the Warsaw (Ind.)*Times-Union* newspaper in the fall of 2001. New material has been added for this publication.

Copyright © 2001 by John J. Davis

Cover design by Kevin Carter

All rights reserved. No part of this book may be reproduced in any form or by any means without written permission of the author. Brief excerpts may be used, however, for published book reviews

Published by: Pinegrove Publishing
                P.O. Box 557
                Winona Lake, IN 46590 USA

Additional copies of this book may be purchased for $1.95 each plus $1.00 for postage and handling from the above address. See pages 43-44 for other books by Dr. Davis.

ISBN 0-9635865-6-4

1

The Origin And History of Islam

There are more than 1.2 billion Muslims in the world, making Islam one of the most significant religions on contemporary landscapes. In fact, they make up one-fifth of the world's population.

Islam is relatively new to the United States but already has 5.3 million followers and is one of the fastest growing religions in America.

In spite of these impressive figures, Islam is largely unknown in our country. Most U.S. citizens catch only snatches of Islamic life through television news reports and, therefore, end up with a myopic vision of this fascinating religion.

The cry of every true Muslim is, "There is no God but Allah, and Muhammad is his prophet." This declaration, which is the heart of Islam, provides us with a clue to its origin. Muhammad was born in A.D. 570 (some say 571 or as late as 580) in Mecca to the Hashim family of the Quaraish tribe. The meaning of his name is "highly praised." Some of the details of his early life are somewhat clouded because no biography was written about him until he had been dead for 100 years. At least four were written during the second century after his death.

His father, Abdallah, died before he was born and his mother passed away when he was six. His paternal grandfather, Abd al-Muttalib, cared for him until his death, then his uncle, Abu Talib, took him in.

With time, Muhammad married and became a man of means and standing in Mecca. His spiritual journey began while he was meditating in a cave outside Mecca in A.D. 610. He fell into a trance and while sweating and trembling, he claimed the angel Gabriel spoke to him. No longer a mere merchant, he now became the prophet of God with a revelation from heaven.

Public Preaching

He began preaching publicly in A.D. 613 and his early message to the people was twofold: (1) There is only one God to whom all must submit, and (2) A future day of judgment is coming when all people will be judged as to whether or not they have followed the laws of God.

Many "revelatory" experiences followed this event and with them came the foundations of modern Islam. Muhammad's stature as a prophet was accepted slowly at first, but his following eventually encompassed large numbers in Mecca. Those committed to his teaching became known as "Muslims" - "those who submit to God" - and the new religion as "Islam," meaning "submission to God."

Early Islam was a movement of young people, mostly under 40 years of age, and from the middle class of Mecca.

The growth and influence of Muhammad's monotheism in Mecca became a source of contention and persecution. Mecca, after all, was a center of polytheistic worship and the sale of idols didn't fare well with monotheistic trends.

The persecution of Muhammad and his followers became so intense by A.D. 622 that they were forced to flee to Yathrib, later called Medina, where they were warmly accepted.

He built his base of power there but in A.D. 630 returned to Mecca, where he and his troops took control without any significant resistance. The city was cleared of its idols and Islam became firmly established.

Both Mecca and Medina became sacred cities to Muslims as well as Jerusalem, where the prophet Muhammad was supposed to have ascended to heaven.

Muhammad died from an ordinary fever in A.D. 632. He had no male heir and no provision had been made for a successor as leader of the Muslim community-state. Abu Bakr, Muhammad's father-in-law and close friend, was chosen by the Meccan Quaraish as the new leader, or caliph.

Abu Bakr ruled for two years and was succeeded by Umar, who was caliph for a decade and during whose rule Islam spread extensively east and west, conquering the Persian Empire, Syria and Egypt.

Historical Interpretation

Depending on what historian you read, this was either a violent military conquest (general historians) or was a more or less peaceful infiltration into new territories and became violent only when infidels resisted or repressed Islam (Islamic historians).

There is little doubt, however, that the Arab conquests behind the spread of Islam were violent overthrows of existing governments and the establishment of Islam as the state religion involved a little more than genteel suggestions.

By A.D. 661 Damascus became the capital of the Islamic world under the Umayyad caliphate. The world of Islam now stretched from the borders of China to southern France. Not only did the Islamic conquests continue during this period through North Africa to Spain and France in the West, but also in parts of Central Asia and countries further east. This was the age when the fundamental religious, social and legal institutions of the newly founded Islamic world were established.

The Abbasids succeeded the Umayyads and moved the capital to Baghdad, which quickly developed into an important center of learning and culture. They ruled the Islamic world for more than 500 years until Hulagu, the Mongol ruler, captured Baghdad in A.D. 1258.

While they were in power, strong dynasties such as the Fatimids, Ayyubids and Mamluks held power in Egypt, Syria and Palestine.

It was during this time that the Crusades were conducted to capture Jerusalem and the surrounding regions for Christianity. The Crusaders held the land of Palestine for a time, but in A.D. 1187, Saladin recaptured Jerusalem and returned it to Muslim rule.

Ottoman Turks

The Ottoman Turks then became the dominant power in the Muslim world and in A.D. 1453, they captured Constantinople and ended the Byzantine Empire. The Ottomans then conquered much of Eastern Europe and nearly the entire Arab world.

The Ottoman Empire came to an end in 1917 as the result of the invading armies of World War I and also because of internal corruption.

Following the war, the British and French took control of the region by secret treaties, which resulted in ruling "mandates." Islam, however, remained firmly entrenched as the dominant religion of the region.

The post World War I colonial rule of these territories has always been remembered with disdain by the Arabs and is often referred to when Arab leaders want to muster the support of Muslim Middle Eastern countries for their cause.

Saddam Hussein, for example, attempted to gain support of the Muslim countries against the United States by claiming he was the victim of a new western colonialism. More recently, we have heard the same language from Osama bin-Ladin of Afghanistan.

One should not think of Islam as a perfectly unified world religion. While there is a large core of commonly held beliefs among Muslims, there are also significant divisions.

Some of these divisions go back to the days immediately following the death of Muhammad.

The largest of these divisions are the Sunnis (with whom Saddam Hussein is identified), while a smaller but no less powerful group are the Shi'ites. The majority of the people of Iran and Iraq are Shi'ite, as are those of Lebanon.

There are a number of Shi'ite splinter groups around the world and they all vary in their interpretation of Islamic theology. The most radical theologically are the so-called Seveners or Ismailites. Today they are found mainly in India, Pakistan and East Africa.

The doctrines and practices of Muslims is a matter of great curiosity among westerners. The next chapter will focus on the teachings of Islam.

2

Islam's Teachings And Practices

With the widely publicized declarations of Muslim extremists calling for holy war (Jihad) against the United States and the Western world, many are wondering just what kind of religion Islam really is.

Remember that it was in the name of Allah, the God of Islam, that terrorists crashed domestic airliners into the Trade Towers in New York City and the Pentagon in Washington, D.C. on Sept. 11, 2001.

The result of this momentous catastrophe in the name of religion has left many Americans wondering what Islam teaches, and to what extent its more than one billion followers practice this kind of theology.

The authority for the Islamic faith resides in four bodies of literature. The most important of these is the Quran, which is believed by them to have been revealed to Mohammad beginning in A.D. 610 while meditating in a cave outside Mecca. The total time of revelation is regarded as 23 years and it was all received in the Arabic language. This book is understood to be the earthly version of that which exists in heaven and, therefore, is referred to as *un-al-kitab* ("Mother of all books").

The Quran is divided into 114 chapters (*suras*) and each chapter contains verses known as *ayat*. Only the Arabic version is regarded as the authoritative word of God by all schools of Islamic thought, and this text contains no variants.

Muslim children are encouraged to memorize the Quran in Arabic, even if this is not the language of their country. It is clear that when Muhammad wrote the Quran, he was deeply influenced by biblical history and theology.

There are many references to biblical personalities and events in the Quran, but often with a different twist.

Additional Law

When certain issues are left undisclosed in the Quran, the Muslims have the *sunnah* and *hadiths* for final authority in their spiritual and social life. The practices and traditions of Islam (*sunnah*) are records of Muhammad's actual life and his sayings (*hadiths*). These were collected and recorded in the early years of Islam.

Also important to the life of the Muslim is a body of religious law called *al-Shari'ah*, which is written in Arabic. This collection of laws helps the Muslim apply the various principles of the Quran.

Between A.D. 750 and A.D. 850 four schools of interpretation of the *Shari'ah* developed. These are not distinctively different schools of theology, but they represent different ways of defining morals and practices.

Mystical traditions in Islam have been preserved in Sufi texts. In an attempt to discover spiritual realities behind the various laws and traditions, Islamic mystics called Sufis appeared in the eighth century and their teachings continue to be a force in parts of Islam today.

So what do Muslims really believe? Central to their faith is the belief in only one God, who in Arabic is known as Allah. Muhammad's notion of monotheism was rooted in ideas which were taught by Judaism, Christianity and some Arabic sects.

While the monotheism of the Muslims has historical roots that are related to Christianity, their definition of God in many important aspects is quite different. For example, the God of Christians is one, but exists in three persons: Father, Son and Holy Spirit. The tri-unity of God is totally foreign to Islamic thought.

The Muslim view of God is focused on His transcendence and absolute power. All theists attribute to God both transcendence (He is above the universe and not limited by it) and imminence (He is present in the world).

The Muslim faith is deeply rooted in what is commonly called theological determinism (*taqdeer*). In other words, God is the absolute ruler of the universe and He determines all that is to happen. The Quran and the Hadith are clear that nothing can happen in the world without the will of God. For most Muslims, this means that everything is predetermined and man is essentially helpless to change anything that occurs in his or her life.

For some in Muslim societies, this can lead to apathy and less than a strong commitment to succeed in business or other enterprises.

But many Muslim clerics, like Christian theologians, struggle with the issue of divine will and human responsibility. The question simply is, "How can God judge an individual for an act he or she could not resist doing?"

Angels and Prophets

Islam believes in the existence of angels and the ministry of prophets. The Quran regards Jesus as a prophet. Even though He was born of a virgin (3:45-47), did many miracles (3:49) and ascended to heaven (4:158), He is not God (5:117).

Muslims believe in a general judgment of both the living and the dead when they will appear before God and be confronted with the deeds done in life. The day when this will occur is unknown.

Each individual will receive a book which records all their deeds. Those who have lived wickedly will receive their book in the left hand (the unclean hand), while those who are righteous will hold their books in their right hands.

Only those who have lived by total submission to Allah's will can expect to survive the judgment.

Heaven is seen as the reward for piety and hell as final punishment for the wicked.

Islam has at its core of belief and behavior five pillars: faith, prayer, care for the needy, self-purification and the pilgrimage to Mecca.

The faith of the Muslim is centered in the word *shahada*, which carries the idea of a confession. At the heart of this is the declaration, "There is no God but Allah, and Muhammad is His prophet."

Prayer (*salat*) is one of the most visible and well-known rituals in Islam. Each Muslim is required to pray five times each day: at sunrise, at noon, in mid-afternoon, at sunset and one hour after sunset. Worshipers may pray anywhere, but when possible, the mosque is preferred.

These five prayers contain verses from the Quran, and they are spoken in Arabic. Provision is made for personal supplication, however, that can be made in one's own language.

Care for the needy (*zakat*) or almsgiving is based on the principle that all things belong to God, and that wealth is, therefore, held by human beings in trust. The word *zakat* means both "purification" and "growth." One's possessions are purified by setting aside a portion for those in need, and like the pruning of plants, this cutting back balances and encourages new growth.

The fast (*sawm*) relates to the month of Ramadan, when all Muslims abstain from food, drink and sexual relations from first light until sundown. This month commemorates the month in which Muhammad received his first revelations. Daylight is defined as that time when a white thread can be distinguished from a black one.

Those who are sick, elderly or on a journey, and women who are pregnant or nursing, are permitted to break the fast and make up an equal number of days later in the year.

The final pillar, the Pilgrimage or *hajj*, is the journey to Mecca which is the obligation of every Muslim who is physically and financially able to go. It is expected that each Muslim will visit Mecca at least once in his or her lifetime. Mecca is the principal holy city of Islam. Medina, where Muhammad is buried, is second, and Jerusalem, where he ascended to heaven, is third.

Ethical Norms

Muslim ethical norms fall into three categories: (1) *fard* - actions that are firm obligations such as obedience to the five pillars of the faith; (2) *haram* - practices that are expressly prohibited, such as idolatry; and (3) *halal* - actions that are permissible.

Both men and women are to dress modestly, but no specific guidelines are given to guide in the selection of special clothes.

Most Muslim tradition in this area is strongly influenced by Arab Middle Eastern cultures.

While some Islamic states require a woman to be partially shrouded (allowing only the eyes to be seen) or completely covered, the Quran does not specify such dress. Women are admonished in the Quran to dress in public in such a way that she does not draw attention to her physical beauty (24:31).

Drinking wine and eating pork are both forbidden in Islam. The Quran allows men to have up to four wives, but this is rarely practiced in most countries because of the high cost of dowries that are required for each wife.

Divorce is allowed in Islam (2:228-242; 115:1-7) and according to the *al-shari'ah*, or religious law, a marriage is dissolved when the husband says, "I divorce you" three times in public. These statements cannot be made at one time, however. The final recitation must wait for a period of three months.

3

Terrorism And The World of Islam

Ugly scenes of terrorist slaughters in the Middle East and elsewhere in the name of Islam have stunned people worldwide.

Is there any cause that justifies blowing up a school bus carrying little children or exploding an airplane filled with innocent travelers?

Does Islam condone or encourage such ruthless behavior?

Since most Americans see only the radical elements in Muslim societies most of the time, their answer would be an unequivocal "yes." But such a conclusion would be both wrong and unfortunate.

I have lived and traveled extensively in the Arab Middle East since 1963 and have had hundreds of contacts with Muslims who clearly abhor such radical behavior and are, as a matter of fact, incensed that these violent acts of human slaughter are done in the name of Allah.

The Arab Muslims I have come to know are peace-loving and just want to raise their families in serene settings and, in general, enjoy life like everyone else.

But they are also first to admit that there are elements in their society that adopt a very aggressive form of Islam in order to give theological justification to their fanatical behavior.

Peaceful Passages

The Quran does, indeed, contain many admonitions to make peace and treat others with civility. For example, if your enemy offers peace, you must treat them accordingly. "Thus, if they let you be, and do not make war on you, and offer you peace, God does not allow you to harm them" (4:90). "If they seek peace, then seek you peace. And trust in God for He is the One that heareth and knoweth all things" (8:61).

Also observed in the Quran is the injunction not to initiate hostilities (2:190). Of course, if you are attacked, you may respond with force. Such hostilities must be brought to a speedy end when the enemy seeks peace (2:192-3).

Instructions to Kill?

While the Quran contains many instructions that would seem to encourage peaceful behavior, there are an equal number of verses that suggest quite the opposite.

Particularly strong are those verses that deal with non-Muslims who are regularly called *kaafir* ("infidels," "rejecters" or "unbelievers"). Take, for example, the injunction of 9:5: "So when the sacred months have passed away, then slay the idolaters wherever you find them, and take them captives and besiege them and lie in wait for them in every ambush, then if they repent and keep up prayer and pay the poor-rate, leave their way free to them; surely Allah is forgiving, merciful."

In *Surah An-Nissa,* verse 76 of the Quran, we read, "Those who believe fight in the cause of Allah, and those who reject Faith fight in the cause of Evil; so fight ye against the friends of Satan; feeble indeed is the cunning of Satan."

It is no semantic accident that the United States is called the "Great Satan" by Muslim extremists. Once Satan is identified, he can be destroyed.

Again, the Quran demands that Believers, "Slay (enemies) wherever you find them!" (4:89). Muslims are encouraged to "Fight them, and Allah will punish them by your hands, cover them with shame, help you (to victory) over them, heal the breasts of Believers." (*Surah At-Touba,* verse 14).

In places, the Quran singles out Christians and Jews for special treatment. "O ye who believe, take not the Jews or Christians for your friends or protectors. They are but friends and protectors to each other." (*Surah Al-Maidah* 5:51). The language of *Sura Al-Taubah* 2:29 is even stronger, "Fight against those who believe not in Allah."

Stirred Passions

It is verses like the above that virtually all radical leaders of Islam have utilized in stirring up the passions of those Muslims who have been convinced the pagan West in general, and the Satanic U.S. in particular, must be destroyed by Jihad. Jihad literally refers to "struggle," but in popular use has the idea of "Holy War."

One need only read the 1998 Fatwah urging Jihad against Americans issued by Osama bin Ladin and others to see how Quranic admonitions are twisted to legitimize terrorism.

The Fatwah is signed not only by Sheikh Osama Bin-Muhammad Bin-Ladin (his full name with title), but also by four other radical political and clerical leaders in the region. This Fatwah has been widely circulated in the Arab world, and especially among West Bank Arabs.

The opening paragraph reads as follows: "Praise be to God, who revealed the Book, controls the clouds, defeats factionalism, and says in His Book, 'But when the forbidden months are past, then fight and slay the pagans wherever you find them, seize them, beleaguer them, and lie in wait for them in every stratagem (of war).'...The Arabian Peninsula has never...been stormed by any forces like the crusader armies now spreading in it like locusts, consuming its riches and destroying its plantations. All this is happening at a time when nations are attacking Muslims like people fighting over a plate of food."

It is important for Osama Bin Ladin to label America's war against terrorism a war against Islam. By doing that, he can invoke the admonitions of the Quran and call for armed conflict against the United States.

Later in this Fatwah he says, "We - with God's help - call on every Muslim who believes in God and wishes to be rewarded to comply with God's order to kill the Americans and plunder their money wherever and whenever they find it."

Common Language

The language of this declaration is common to all radical clerics and terrorist leaders within Islam who are not just committed to the purity of Islamic truth, but to its supremacy in all cultures.

It is true, of course, that most Muslim leaders, both clerical and governmental, would not ascribe to the language of this Fatwah.

But such declarations (and there have been many of them during the past 10 years) put moderate Arab/Muslim leaders in an awkward position.

While they would like to condemn such proposals publicly, they rarely do for the simple reason they do not want to be perceived as opposing Islamic causes.

What most Americans do not understand is that Islam is not just a mere religion that one celebrates one day a week then forgets it the rest of the week (as many church people do). It is a culture, a life, a philosophy, a government and a world view. The dream of every Muslim is to live under Islamic rule that perpetuates all the principles of the Quran.

A Common Interpretation

Now, to be fair, I should point out that

most clerics here in America and Mullahs I have met in the Middle East do not interpret these admonitions to violence and war in a universal way. They insist that they were written for a time when Muslims were being persecuted by the pagans in the region of Mecca. It was the Muslim state in Medina that was to take up arms, not individual citizens.

Moiz Amjad writes in *Understanding Islam* that, "The pagans against whom fighting is ordained by the referred verses are not general in nature, but are actually only the polytheists of Banu Ishmael."

In other words, while the peace admonitions of the Quran are universal, the militaristic ones are specific and local. That might fly among moderate Muslims, but ones I know in the West Bank in Ramalla debunk that interpretation.

As Helmi Musa put it, "If the laws of the Quran relating to peace are universal, so are the commands for war and Jihad. The issue in the Quran is not just against local tribes or sects in Arabia, but against Infidels everywhere. The categories of Believers (Muslims) and Infidels (everyone else) are universal." (The parentheses are mine).

Radical Muslim terrorists have made the word Jihad to mean, "killing your enemy using any means, whatsoever." This clearly takes the term out of the context of the Quran. First, Jihad can only be declared by a Muslim state, not by individuals, and second, the purpose for which Jihad can be called is only to fight against persecution.

No Legal Force

Thus, the many Jihads called by terrorist leaders do not have true Islamic legal force. Unfortunately, however, most impoverished and beleaguered Arabs do not know that.

They are told a thousand times over that they are being oppressed by western infidels who want to crush Islam. Their enemies are "colonial powers" who are polluting Islam's sacred lands just as the colonial powers did after World War I.

While Americans should recognize that most Moslems are not violent terrorists, it would be foolhardy to ignore the rapidly growing minority that are prone to a distorted interpretation of the Quran.

Americans should be alert to this small minority just as we would be alert to the radical and often violent activities of the Aryan Nation or Ku Klux Klan who like to display crosses and quote verses from the Bible.

One other observation would be appropriate here. It must be acknowledged that the Quran, unlike any other religious literature, is more easily twisted to encourage the violent overthrow of existing "Infidel governments."

How else can one explain Muslim violent behavior in the Philippines, the Baltic States, North Africa, Indonesia, the Middle East and Central Asia? With rare exceptions, terrorists and insurrectionists are connected with some form of Islam.

Also, most Muslim governments are not democracies and often establish oppressive and non-tolerant policies (Iran, Saudi Arabia, Afghanistan, Sudan, Yemen, the United Arab Emirates and Iraq, for example).

This, of course, does not make all Muslims insurrectionists or terrorists, nor does it justify criminal behavior against people of Middle Eastern descent. But it does acknowledge there is a worldwide movement of Muslim extremists who will use any means to overthrow governments to establish Islamic rule.

In the long run, it will not be the bombs of the United States or England that will stem this tide of terrorism in the name of Islam, but strong rejection of such terror by the millions of peace-loving Muslims around the world.

They must stand against the radicalization of their faith just as Christians have been required to denounce racial terrorists who burn black churches then claim to be fighting for the interests of Christ.

It is interesting that during days and even weeks following the tragic destruction of the Trade Towers in New York, the strong condemnation of the Muslim terrorists on the part of Islamic leaders and clerics around the world has been but a whisper. Or when it has come as a denunciation, it was with some qualification such as, "Of course, one must recognize that it is American foreign policy or American moral decadence that brought all this about." These qualifications leave the impression that such condemnations are not entirely genuine.

If a group of radical Christians hijacked airplanes and flew them into large hotels in Mecca, there would be a strong condemnation on the part of Christians world-wide. Without qualification pastors and priests alike, would denounce such senseless acts.

When terrorist organizations are harbored and, in many cases, supported by Islamic countries, it does raise questions as to the moral commitment of Islam to condemn and punish those who slaughter innocent civilians.

Some of the victims have been Muslims while others "Infidels." In any case, the moral character of the act is the same and should be soundly condemned.

4

Islam And The Land of Palestine

To whom does the land of Palestine belong? Should it be called Israel rather than Palestine?

Why has this relatively barren, rocky and desolate land been the object of such passionate debate --- and war?

These and hundreds of similar questions swirl above the landscapes of this tiny strip of land that borders the east side of the Mediterranean Sea.

To understand the furor of the current conflict, several things need to be remembered. First, passions over territory run much deeper in the Middle East than elsewhere because the very identity of a people is inseparably related to their ancestral homeland.

Second, both Jews and Arabs have a long history of occupation in the land. They are both descendants of Abraham, who visited the land first in 2090 B.C., and both claim historic rights to that land.

The Arabs are the descendants of Ishmael, who was the son of Abraham by the Egyptian maid, Hagar (Gen.16:1-4,16). Ishmael's descendants were promised to be numerous and great people (Gen.16:10-12).

The Jews, on the other hand, are the descendants of Isaac, who was the son of Abraham by his wife, Sarah (Gen. 21:1-8). It was to him the land of Canaan was promised by covenant (Gen. 17:19 cf. 13:15, 17; 15:7) and reaffirmed in promises to King David (2 Sam. 7:10-16).

The "land of promise" was to encompass all the territory from the "River of Egypt" to the Euphrates River (Gen. 15:18; Josh. 1:4). Never did the Hebrews ever occupy all that land leading many biblical scholars to conclude that this prophecy will be fulfilled in the future.

Joshua's Conquest

In 1405 B.C. the Hebrew armies under

Joshua conquered vast portions of the land after 7-1/2 years of war. Thus, Jews will argue that Palestine is their land by both covenant and conquest.

But the Hebrews were defeated by two enemies later and many of the people were taken captive. In 722 B.C. Assyrian soldiers crushed Samaria, the capital of the Northern Kingdom of Israel, after a three-year siege.

Jerusalem, the capital of the southern kingdom, fell to the Babylonians in 586 B.C. and many Jews were taken captive to Babylon.

While some returned from exile 70 years later, their presence was but a shadow of the past.

Israel as a political entity had come to an end, but the land of Israel (later called Palestine) continued as their homeland. In the centuries that followed, however, the Jews suffered under the military and political power of the Persians, Greeks and Romans.

When Jerusalem fell to the Romans in A.D. 70, Israel as a true homeland came to an end.

Jews since have been scattered among the nations, an event commonly referred to as the Diaspora.

Some Jews, of course, remained in the land and their descendants have survived to the present day.

The land fell to Byzantine control from A.D. 324 to A.D. 638. This was followed by the sweeping conquests of the Muslim Arabs, who dominated the land from A.D. 638 to A.D. 1456.

The Ottoman Turks held sway in Palestine from A.D. 1456 until the end of World War 1(1918). From 1922 until 1947 Palestine was under the British Mandate.

As you can see, this strip of land has been contested for three millennia and the end is not in sight!

The Balfour Declaration

At the outbreak of war in 1914, Zionists (whose goal it was to establish a homeland in Palestine) began to put pressure on the British to establish a state for them in Palestine. They eventually enjoyed some success when Lord Balfour wrote the following to Lord Rothschild on Nov. 2, 1917: "His Majesty's Government views with favour the establishment in Palestine a national home for the Jewish people and will use their best endeavours to facilitate the achievement of this object, it being clearly understood that nothing shall be done which may prejudice the civil and religious rights of existing non-Jewish communities in Palestine or the rights and political status enjoyed by Jews in any other country."

This declaration had the blessing of the British Cabinet as well as that of President Wilson. Later, France and Italy gave their approval.

The Arab world, however, angrily denounced the declaration and vowed to prevent any such thing from occurring. Thus began the Middle East problem!

The declaration sparked Zionist fervor in Europe and many Jews began to immigrate to Palestine. British governors, working under the Mandate, attempted to mediate what was a rapidly growing problem between resident Arabs and the large numbers of immigrant Jews.

Even though under a British Mandate,

the Muslim Arabs considered Palestine as their land, which they had conquered in A.D. 638.

The seeds of the modern conflict over the land were sown at this time. Jews purchased large portions of the land and by 1947 had significant holdings in the Jezreel Valley in the north as well as land along the Mediterranean.

Serious conflicts broke out between Jews and Arabs, so the General Assembly of the United Nations voted on Nov.19, 1947, to partition Palestine, giving the Jews a small portion of the land. On May 14, 1948, Israel was declared a nation.

The Arabs in the land fiercely resisted this move. War broke out, and Jewish fighters seized additional land. This led to the displacement of many Arabs.

The Arab attacks on Israel in 1967 and 1973 were attempts to end the Jewish state and drive the Jews off the land completely. Both attempts failed and many more Arab refugees were created, especially when the West Bank was captured from Jordan in 1967.

These thousands of Arab refugees have not been assimilated into surrounding Arab lands, but have been kept in large refugee camps supported largely by United Nations funds. It is in these camps that bitter hatred of Israel has been fostered, and it is here that the various terrorist organizations have had their most successful recruitment.

Right to the Land

The right to the land of Palestine has been variously argued. The Jews say the land was promised to their father Abraham, it was conquered by the Hebrews under Joshua and has been occupied by various numbers of Jews ever since.

The Arabs remember the great Muslim conquests of A.D. 638 and their presence in the land since that date. They too argue they are the descendants of Abraham and, therefore, have land rights.

Of course, much of the intellectual battle centers over who was in the land first. Jews trace their earliest presence there in the person of Abraham, which would go back to 2090 B.C.

Not to be outdone, Arab revisionist

historians and archaeologists are now claiming that the Palestinian Arabs are really descendants of the Canaanites, who, of course, were there before Abraham arrived in 2090 B.C.

Archaeologist Jala Kazzouh, for example, has been digging at Tel Sofar near the modern city of Nablus. He found Middle Bronze I (2100-1800 B.C.) Canaanite ruins at the site and declared, "This establishes our roots in the land. We're saying these are our ancestors and these are our roots."

Neat, but no sale! No competent historian or archaeologist would take seriously the notion that the modern Arabs in the land are descendants of the Middle Bronze Age Canaanites. Arab roots are in Arabia, not Palestine.

When you hear the phrase, "Palestinian Arab," it merely means the individual was born in the land of Palestine. Many of the Arabs living in the land, however, are not Palestinian Arabs, but Jordanian, Syrian or Egyptian Arabs by birth.

Present Situation

There is serious unrest among the Arabs in the West Bank and most harbor a bitter hatred for Israel (and the United States). Almost daily there are vicious attacks on Israelis by Islamic terrorists.

Israel, in good old-fashioned Middle Eastern tradition, responds with military power and usually at a greater scale. ("We pay back with interest," one Israeli explained to me.)

Death, carnage and heartbreak are, therefore, part of everyday life on both sides of the border.

Terrorist organizations like Hamas, Hizballah, Al-Jihad, Fata, The Palestine Liberation Front, Popular Front for the Liberation of Palestine and the Palestine Islamic Jihad are active all along the West Bank and in Lebanon.

Islamic radicals in the West Bank and elsewhere have been willing to commit suicide for their cause and this practice has raised questions about its acceptability in light of the Quran's teaching.

According to clerical interpretation of

the Quran, suicide is forbidden and implies a lack of trust in God. When a Muslim commits suicide, he declares that he does not believe that God knows about his sufferings.

However, Muslim clerics are quick to point out that there may be occasions when suicide is acceptable. If a legal Jihad has been declared and a suicide bomber is fighting as a part of "war" against an "oppressor," then he is not really a disobedient follower, but a martyr who will receive quick access to heaven.

It is interesting that Arab extremists, like Saddam Hussein, Osama bin Laden and many living in the West Bank, have now moved away from making this conflict one for Arab land. It is now a battle for Islamic land and these groups claim they are attempting to recover the territories from the infidels (the U.S. and Israel).

The purpose of these proclamations is to involve more of the Muslim world in the conflict. Only 18 percent of the Muslims in the world are Arab; the rest represent a wide variety of nationalities.

Unless something very unusual occurs,

the bitterness, violence, distrust and hatred are likely to continue.

What are the immediate chances for true peace in the region? Virtually nonexistent. What can Americans do in light of this tragedy in the land of Jesus' birth? The Psalmist give us the best advice: "Pray for the peace of Jerusalem" (Psalm 122:6).

Additional Publications by the Author

Books

Israel: From Conquest to Exile. A Commentary on Joshua and 2 Kings, 542 pages. (Co-authored with John C. Whitcomb)

Paradise to Prison: Studies in Genesis. 384 pages.

Moses and the Gods of Egypt: Studies in Exodus. 350 pages.

Conquest and Crisis: Studies in Joshua, Judges and Ruth. 176 pages.

Biblical Numerology: A Basic Study of the Use of Numbers in the Bible. 174 pages.

The Birth of a Kingdom: Studies in 1 and 2 Samuel and 1 Kings 1-11. 209 pages.

The Mummies of Egypt. 143 pages.

What About Cremation? A Christian Perspective. 136 pages.

The Perfect Shepherd: Studies in the Twenty-third Psalm. 160 pages.

Contemporary Counterfeits: A Practical and Biblical Evaluation of Occultism. 43 pages.

Demons, Exorcism and the Evangelical. 16 pages.

The Dead Sea Scrolls. 15 pages.

Islam, Terrorism and The Middle East. 44 pages.

Real Fishermen Are Never Thin. 123 pages.

Real Fishermen Never Lie. 124 pages.

Real Fishermen Never Wear Suits. 121 pages.

Favorite Fish & Seafood Recipes. 223 pages.

A Lake Guide to Fishing and Boating in Kosciusko County, Indiana. 93 pages.

Chart

Hebrew Verb Chart: An Analysis of the Strong Verb.

Cassette Tape Sets

Conquest and Settlement, 12 Tapes and Syllabus (24 lectures)

The United Monarchy, 12 Tapes and Syllabus (24 lectures)

Video Cassette

Basics of Bass Fishing. A 35-minute color video.

To receive a free complete catalog and ordering information, write Pinegrove Publishing, P.O. Box 557, Winona Lake, IN 46590.